WALKING *on* HIGH HEELS

by Peggy Pedroza

bush
PUBLISHING
& associates

WWW.BUSHPUBLISHING.COM

Walking on High Heels: What Do You Do When Life Takes You Down a Road You Never Expected?
ISBN: 978-0-9967285-4-6
Copyright © 2015 by Peggy Pedroza

Bush Publishing & Associates books may be ordered at www.bushpublishing.com or www.amazon.com.

For further information, please contact:
Bush Publishing & Associates
www.bushpublishing.com

Table of Contents

Habakkuk 3:19 (NKJV), The Lord God is my strength; He will make my feet like deer's feet, And He will make me walk on my high hills.

Habakkuk 3:19 (AMP), The Lord GOD is my strength [my source of courage, my invincible army]; He has made my feet [steady and sure] like hinds' feet and makes me walk [forward with spiritual confidence] on my high places [of challenge and responsibility].

Foreword

Speaking words of faith has been at the forefront of our lives for years and we were seeing the fruit of it—our family was happy, life was going well and everything was falling into place. But in one moment, our lives changed and we stepped onto a path we never saw coming. I got a call that Peggy had been in a four-wheeler accident and it was not good. I didn't know what we were about to walk into but on the inside, I had a peace and a calm.

Negative thoughts did try to come and questioning why. Had we done something or *not* done something that allowed the enemy to attack or was it because we were in the will of God? Either way, I felt angry. But I knew not to be moved by what I felt—or saw.

I remember looking at her chart late one night after the surgery. It read, *quadriplegic.* I knew this wasn't going to be easy and that it would take all we had to survive it. But no matter what was written on the chart, I was not accepting it. This was *my* wife.

Over the following weeks, I searched the scriptures. When I came across certain ones, the Holy Spirit would quicken them to me. I knew it was what I needed or what Peggy would need. He took me to Proverbs 4:20-22, Isaiah 58:8 and James 1:2-4. Then He took me to Mark 11:23, *For verily I say unto you, that **whosoever shall say unto this mountain, be thou removed, and be thou cast into the sea;** and shall not doubt in his heart, but shall believe that those things which he saith shall come to pass; he shall have whatsoever he saith.* He told me that the sea was big and it could handle our mountain. Big mountain—Big sea.

Of all that we have gone through, His love for us has never failed; it has not and will not ever run out. Nothing can ever separate us from His love. He has not forgotten us. Because of Him, our family is *still happy*, life is *still going well* and everything is *still falling into place.*

The worst is never the worst. There's always HOPE!

—Mike Pedroza, Peggy's husband

It's a Good Thing to Hope for Help from God

I'll never forget the trouble, the utter lostness,
the taste of ashes, the poison I've swallowed.
I remember it all—oh, how well I remember—
the feeling of hitting the bottom.
But there's one other thing I remember,
and remembering, I keep a grip on hope:

God's loyal love couldn't have run out,
his merciful love couldn't have dried up.
They're created new every morning.
How great your faithfulness!
I'm sticking with God (I say it over and over).
He's all I've got left.

God proves to be good to the man who passionately waits,
to the woman who diligently seeks.
It's a good thing to quietly hope,
quietly hope for help from God.
It's a good thing when you're young
to stick it out through the hard times.

When life is heavy and hard to take,
go off by yourself. Enter the silence.
Bow in prayer. Don't ask questions:
Wait for hope to appear.
Don't run from trouble. Take it full-face.
The "worst" is never the worst.
—Lamentations 3:19-30 MSG

Introduction

We can go through life so fast that we forget to be thankful for the simplest things. I know. I did it for years. Life will pass you by if you're not careful—taking the simple things for granted right along with it. But those simple things are sometimes the most important. Like rolling over in bed, walking across a room, drinking from a cup or holding a pen. Those things come as natural to us as breathing. That is, until they're gone. That's when you realize how precious they really were.

Have you ever thought, *"That could never happen to me!"* I'm sure most everyone has sometime in their lives. But what if something were to happen? Something so unexpected.

Life can change in an instant and take you down an entirely different road than you ever expected. And you have a choice to make. Are you going to let it get the best of you? Defeat you? Define you? Or will you meet it head on with a confidence in knowing that everything *really is* going to be all right?

We hear testimonies of people who overcame huge obstacles. We hear the beginning and the great victory at the end...but what about the middle? How did they get through it? How did they walk it out? It's one thing to hear the outcome but an entirely different thing to walk through it with them.

As you read this book, I invite you to do just that. And I pray that it will encourage you in your own walk of faith.

CHAPTER 1

THE REPORT

Isaiah 53:1(NKJV), Who has believed our report?
And to whom has the arm of the Lord been revealed?

L ying motionless, my brother crawled over to make sure I was all right. The four-wheeler that we were riding in just moments before was now overturned on top of me with the roll bar lying across my neck and shoulder. He tried to lift it off but could only move it a few inches and it wouldn't go any higher. "Can you slide out from under it?" he asked, but there was only a stunned look on my face and no response. Then he gave out and couldn't hold it any longer. He tried to let it down slowly, hoping that either I, or the four-wheeler, was in a slightly different position. Neither had changed. As he let it down, my eyes opened wide and he could tell it was hurting me. He lifted it back up a few inches but still it wouldn't go any higher. He was terrified and didn't know what to do. We were alone, with no phones and we were too far away for anyone to hear if he yelled for help.

At this point, there was nothing he could do. He couldn't pick it up any higher and he couldn't let it go because it was pressing down on me. All he could do was stand there holding the four-wheeler and pray. "Please help me, God! I can't do it! There's no one here to help. Please, God, let me pick it up! You've got to!" He put everything he had left in the next attempt to lift it off of me. The 1000+ pound four-wheeler that he didn't have the strength to hold just moments before, rose up, went right over and stood upright.

Psalm 91:15, He shall call upon Me, and I will answer him: I will be with him in trouble; I will deliver him, and honor him.

My brother was talking to a friend about it later. He said, "Some people would say that adrenalin kicked in and gave me the strength to lift the four-wheeler."

His friend told him, "If it had been adrenalin, you would have lifted it off of her the first two times you tried."

We have an awesome God!

I don't remember the four-wheeler being on top of me and I don't know how long I was out before I regained consciousness. He began assessments, touching my arms, legs and feet, asking if I could move. I was only able to lift my arms slightly. From the chest down, everything was completely still.

I started praying and thanking Jesus over and over for taking care of me while my brother stayed by my side praying. He went back to checking me over. There was a space between my neck and the ground so he gently slid my shoe that was lying beside me in the space to keep my head and neck secure. He asked if I would be all right while he ran to our grandmother's house to call for help. I told him I would and he said he would be right back.

Scripture after scripture would come up in my spirit and I would speak them out loud. *God has not given me a spirit of fear, but of power, love and a sound mind…No weapon formed against me shall prosper…He shall give His angels charge over me.* And when I had prayed all that I knew to pray, I prayed in the spirit.

> *Romans 8:26-27 (NKJV), Likewise the Spirit also helps in our weaknesses. For we do not know what we should pray for as we ought, but the Spirit Himself makes intercession for us with groanings which cannot be uttered. Now He who searches the hearts knows what the mind of the Spirit is, because He makes intercession for the saints according to the will of God.*

There was such a peace that came over me! I knew God was with me and that His angels had protected me. I wasn't anxious or in fear but the longer I lay there…*not* moving…I began to realize that I may need a little more help than I had thought to get out of there. *And*…this may require a little more than a Band-Aid or two!

The word *paralyzed* really didn't come to mind. "Temporarily stunned"…*maybe.* Definitely not paralyzed! I mean, something as serious as being paralyzed *could never happen to me!* Right? After all, I grew up in the country with three brothers! Two older and one younger. That alone will make a girl tough! I've done things growing up that I *probably* shouldn't have. Okay, things I *know* I shouldn't have! And I survived. Falling and being thrown from things was *not* new to me. So why should being thrown from a four-wheeler be any different?

I couldn't move my body but my legs had a strange sensation as if they were suspended in mid-air. I felt like I was still in a sitting position, even though I was lying on my back.

One thing about our family is that sometimes we can find the funniest things in some *not-so-funny* situations. (The more you read, you'll see what I mean!) This was one of those times because this thought came to me. "If I'm going to heaven today then I must be going feet first!" Then I thought about how some people have had near death experiences and saw angels so I looked around… *just in case*…but no one else was there. At least no one that I could see! Anyway…I knew that I hadn't finished my course on the earth and the only way I was getting out of there that day was probably going to be by ambulance. So I began to pray again.

My brother ran as fast as he could up the hill. He ran so hard that he could barely breathe and his whole body hurt. His back was hurt in the accident so that made it even harder. He almost fell before reaching the house from running such a long distance, still praying the whole way there. He ran in the house, called his wife and told her we had been in a wreck and it was very serious.

He told her where we were and to call 9-1-1 and then he hung up.

I could hear him running back to me from a distance and calling my name. I knew he was worried about me; not knowing what to expect when he got back, so I called out to him to let him know I was all right. He was glad to hear my voice and I was just as glad to hear his. He told me that help was on the way and then we prayed some more. Actually, I don't think either of us ever stopped praying.

When the 9-1-1 call went out, local family and friends heard the call over their scanners and rushed to help. But the communications were messed up, and not knowing our exact location, people were combing the woods looking for us.

I was listening carefully for the sound of voices, vehicles, sirens; anything as a sign that help was arriving. "Can you hear the sirens, yet? How long before help gets here?" He replied, "They're coming. Everything's going to be all right. Just stay awake with me."

I had landed on top of an ant mound and fire ants were crawling on my midsection and arms. He was continually wiping them off of me before they could get through my clothes. He had to because I couldn't be moved. He just kept wiping ants and asking if I could move anything yet. I couldn't.

After about thirty minutes, we heard the sound of horns coming from the direction of the creek. He ran to the top of the hill and began shouting as loud as he could to let them know where we were. Then I could hear voices in the distance as people started arriving. I heard my sister-in-law calling out and running toward us. When she reached me, I asked her if she had her cell phone and to call my pastor and explain what had happened. Then I asked her to call my husband, Mike. He was in Kansas City and I wanted him to know what had happened.

By this time, everyone knew where we were. First responders had arrived and began making assessments. I lay there, still calm, answering their questions. I couldn't move but I could tell them where they were touching my legs and toes.

While they were working on me, I was listening for a siren. It didn't seem to take very long before I heard an ambulance in the distance. Just as I did, a helicopter flying overhead drowned out the sound. The ambulance circled the driveway at my grandmother's house but couldn't get to us from any direction so they had to send the medical technicians in a game warden's truck.

I don't remember very much after that, only bits and pieces. One thing that I *do* remember well was someone cutting away the new denim jacket Mike had just given me for Christmas and my favorite pants! I almost asked them to take them off but I kept quiet. There were a lot more important things in life…as I was about to find out.

They put a neck brace on me and put me on a board to be transported. They placed me in the back of the game warden's truck and drove me to the field behind my brother's house about a mile away. I could hear a helicopter in the distance, getting louder and louder the closer we got. Then it dawned on me that the helicopter I heard earlier was there for me. I wanted to ask if they *really* needed to go to all that trouble. Surely, an ambulance would be fine. But I must have been heavily medicated because by then, I really didn't care what they did anymore!

My cousin, who is a paramedic, heard the 9-1-1 call on his scanner. He didn't know who had been hurt, only that it must be family by the location that was given. He called the EMS and had a helicopter put on standby. He hung up but called right back and dispatched them to the scene, not knowing what was wrong or if they were even needed. I am so thankful he did!

After a few more minutes of medical attention, they lifted me from the truck and carried me toward the helicopter. I could feel the heat and wind blowing from it as I was being loaded. Then we lifted off.

I was told later that there were vehicles *everywhere* along the road to my brother's house. My mom tried to get to where I was being loaded on the helicopter but she couldn't get through, so my nephew drove her straight to the hospital instead. We were about an hour from the hospital and they made it there before the helicopter! She told me later what she prayed. "God, she's Your daughter. I can't do anything. I need You to take care of her." He did.

The last two things I remembered were the hospital ceiling lights flashing above me like you see in the movies, and in the emergency room, I could hear and see two doctors across the room discussing how dangerous four-wheelers are. I wanted to tell them we weren't driving crazy, but I was helpless. The medication kept me in and out of consciousness for days, which was probably a good thing.

Family and friends had filled the emergency room waiting area and were lined up and down the hallways. Hearing about all the people that came for support and encouragement for me and my family meant so much to us, especially after finding out how serious it really was. One of my sisters-in-law had asked about my condition and was told that from the look of the x-rays, *she'll never walk again.*

I've heard some amazing stories of things people have witnessed in bad situations and I think that's why I go back to that day, wondering if I might have missed something.

I knew God was right there with me and I had no doubt that He would deliver me out of whatever had just happened. But what *had* just happened? Do you know...I didn't ask that question. Usually, if something blindsides you like that, the first thing you do is try to wrap your thoughts around it. "What happened? Where am I?" I've had my vehicle rear-ended a couple of times and had those thoughts. But I didn't have those thoughts that day. I couldn't have known what happened. I didn't even know we were about to wreck because the last thing I remembered was bouncing up in the seat. Then I was lying on the ground like someone had carefully laid me down on my back. I had a broken neck, broken collarbone and broken shoulder blade and no pain at all. Not even a headache. And no memory of what happened in between those two moments. It was like God just took me out of the situation. And I had absolutely no idea that morning that my life was about to be changed.

I had taken our daughters, Michelle and Allie, to school that morning. I had the day off, so I went back home to study for our church ladies meeting that I was scheduled to teach at the next week. As I was studying, three words came up in my spirit: earnestly, fervently and heartily. I looked them up in the concordance and found this scripture:

James 5:16 KJV, ...The effective fervent prayer of a righteous man avails much.

And the Amplified version: *...The earnest (heartfelt, continued) prayer of a righteous man makes tremendous power available [dynamic in its working].*

I was telling my pastor about this while I was in the hospital and he told me that God had given him the same scripture when he was praying for me.

After I finished studying, I cleaned my house and got ready to pick up the girls from school. We had family visiting from Georgia that week and the girls wanted to see their cousins before they had to travel back home. Mike was in Kansas City on business, so it seemed to be the best day to get them together.

I picked up the girls from school and drove to my mom's house. Later that evening, Mom and I were cooking supper for the family. All of the kids were outside and I heard my brother drive by the house on his four-wheeler. It had been a while since I had seen him, and I was listening for him so I could catch him on his way back. I heard the four-wheeler coming down the road and ran out of the house. I'm not even sure if I told Mom where I was going.

He stopped in front of the house, but before I reached him, one of my nephews and his friend had jumped in the back. They had ridden earlier so, me, *being the adult*, told them it was my turn and they could ride after me. I wanted to visit with my brother. I went to put the seatbelt on but it was broken. Since I didn't have one, he took his off. We weren't going to be riding fast anyway.

We went through trails he had made through the woods, talking and enjoying the scenery. That is, until we got to that last turn. We went around a curve and over a terrace. I remember bouncing up in the seat but don't remember coming back down. What happened next was told to me later.

We weren't going that fast because we had just gone around a curve and hadn't had time to gain a lot of speed. But the speed we were going at was just enough to cause us to land directly in the face of the next terrace. The four-wheeler bucked upward and sideways causing us to be ejected. I went off the side and he went forward over the steering wheel. It had struck a hole that broke the bead seal on the back tire causing it to come off of the rim. With the sideways motion of the four-wheeler and the back tire off, it tipped over, landing with the roll bar across my shoulder and neck.

THE SURGERY

The accident occurred on February 21, 2007. Mike arrived from the airport the following day, just before the surgery. He took our daughter, Michelle, and my mom into my room with him while he prayed over me until they came to get me.

Shortly after surgery, he put earphones on me with Brother Kenneth E. Hagin's CD, *Healing Scriptures,* playing continually. He gave orders for the earphones to stay on and kept me constantly saturated in the Word of God.

OPERATIVE REPORT

Patient: Pedroza, Peggy Caskey
Date: 02/22/2007
BRIEF HISTORY: All-terrain vehicle rollover with cervical spine, left clavicle and left scapula fractures. Spinal cord injury. Complete occlusion of the right vertebral artery. Fractures involving C5, 6 and 7 with jumped facet on the right side of C6 and C7. Initially placed on cervical traction for better alignment. Given the nature of the injury with the amount of damage on the neurological exam, proceeded to decompress as well as stabilize the fractures and subluxations. Risks included but not limited to infection, bleeding, stroke, paralysis, coma and death

were discussed with the family members. Lateral mass screws were placed from C5-C7 on each side. To prevent the risk of injury to the left-side vertebral artery, shorter length mass screws were used on the left. A titanium rod was cut and put over the screws.

Discharge diagnosis—incomplete C6 quadriplegia.

I don't remember asking about my prognosis. I mean, I knew my neck was broken but in my mind it was, "Okay, but can you just go ahead and patch me up so I can go home now? I have things I need to be doing." When Mike told me I would be in the hospital for a while, I couldn't believe it.

I wasn't concerned so much about the prognosis. I trusted God. He had taken care of so many other things and I knew this time wouldn't be any different. And I trusted Mike. He told me everything was going to be all right and that was enough for me. I knew he would let me know what I needed to know, and there were some things he didn't think I needed to know. The prognosis was one of them. I didn't find out what it was until months later when I read it in an article written about Mike in the *Bassmaster* fishing magazine. He had won fifth place in the Bassmaster Central Open on the Red River and they interviewed him after the tournament. He mentioned what this win meant to him and his family and what we had been through. He told them that before the surgery, I had a 10% chance of ever walking again. After surgery, I was given a 40% chance of walking in the first year. Four months after the accident, I was at that fishing tournament weigh-in on a walker.

Was I upset that he kept it from me? Not one bit. If he thought it was relevant, he would have told me. He wasn't receiving a bad report any more than I would have if I had known. He told me exactly what I needed to know—the truth—that everything was going to be all right.

One day, I asked him about the hospital bills. I knew they were piling up because I had been in the hospital for so long. He said, "It's not your concern. Don't think about it. Just focus on your healing."

I was discharged from the hospital nine days later on March 2nd to a rehab hospital. I don't think I ever really grasped how serious it was until Mike told me I would need to be there for at least two months. Regardless of what it looked like, we were going to get through this together and I was going to walk out of that hospital.

Isaiah 53:1(NKJV), Who has believed our report? And to whom has the arm of the Lord been revealed?

1 Peter 2:24 (NKJV), who Himself bore our sins in His own body on the tree, that we, having died to sins, might live for righteousness—by whose stripes you were healed.

We shall believe the report of the Lord.

CHAPTER 2

A VERY PRESENT HELP

Psalm 46:1 (NKJV) God is our refuge and strength, a very present help in trouble.

We all go through storms in life but it's up to us *how* we go through them.

Isaiah 40:31, But they that wait upon the Lord shall renew their strength; they shall mount up with wings as eagles; they shall run, and not be weary; and they shall walk, and not faint.

One of the Hebrew meanings in the Strong's Concordance for *'they shall mount up'* is *'go up over.'* We can focus on the storm and even stay right in the middle of it if we want to. Or we can choose to *go up over*. I went through a lot, but the things that stood out to me the most were the times I chose to *go up over*.

COUNT IT ALL JOY

James 1:2 says to *count it all joy when you fall into various trials,* so it must be possible to find some kind of joy in the middle of your trials. Right?

After surgery, one of my best friends stayed the night with me. She tried washing my hair to get out all the dirt, twigs and who knows what else was knotted in the back of it, but with me lying down and wearing a neck brace, she wasn't very successful. Plus, my hair felt like *things* could still be in there! Sometime during the night, I woke up to what felt like something running back and forth really fast across the back of my head. We were laughing so hard about what could be in my hair, half afraid that something might actually jump out at us! Imagine that! Laughing in the Intensive Care Unit! It must have only been a nerve reacting because she couldn't find anything.

My legs were continually having spasms and I would have to get someone to rub them to make it stop. One night I woke her up to rub my legs, *again,* and apologized *again* for having to wake her. I was in a joint ICU room and there was nowhere for visitors to sleep except in a straight chair. I felt so bad for waking her but she said, "Honey, I didn't come here to sleep. I came here to take care of you."

I couldn't hold anything, so I had to depend on someone else to read to me. I was looking at the blank walls one day and thought that would be a really good place to hang posters with scriptures. My girls were staying the night with the daughter of one of my other best friends, so I sent word for the three girls to each make a poster for me.

One of the scriptures was Nehemiah 8:10, *the joy of the Lord is my strength.* I was staring at that poster one day. I needed strength but I really needed joy, too. So I asked God to help me find some joy in the middle of all this.

You really don't see people laughing who are going through therapy. It's tough work! And to be honest, learning how to do *everything* all over again is not fun. There is no way it was that difficult the first time around! But I was determined to "count it all joy" so I asked God to give me something to laugh at. I *needed* to laugh. And He answered me right away.

On my next trip to the gym for physical therapy, we started working on my sitting balance which means I had to learn how to sit up without falling over. They transferred me from the wheelchair to the physical therapy table with a sliding board. My PT went to move the wheelchair out of the way, but the bag on my catheter was tangled up in the wheels. The wheel rolled over the bag and it started leaking. I looked down at the floor and before I even had time to think, I said, "You just made me pee on the floor." After we got through laughing, we went back to work.

Mom was watching me in therapy one day as I gave everything I had to roll over on my side. After a long struggle, over I went. I told her triumphantly, "If you missed any of my firsts when I was a baby, you're getting a second chance! I just rolled over for the first time!"

I was told there was a possibility that I would have to be catheterized indefinitely. For the rest of my life! This was something that I refused to come to grips with, especially after they made me watch the how-to-video. In the meantime, it had to be done.

Mike was with me one day when my nurse was about to catheterize me. She asked him if he wanted to learn how to put a catheter in. He said, "Sure, if I get my own gloves." The gloves she had were too small so she left out to get him his own box of gloves. I wanted to say, "Wait a minute! Are you seriously going to let him do this? Can't we all just sit down and talk about this first?" But she was out the door, and before I knew it, he was standing there with gloves on…ready to go. I don't know about you, but that can make you raise "both" eyebrows! I mean, don't you at least need a degree to do something like this?

She talked him through how to sterilize everything, carefully going over each step. Then he stopped…looked up at me with his gloved hands in the air like he was about to perform major surgery and said in a serious doctor tone, "Take a deep breath...I'm going in." It's not like I could go anywhere, so after I stopped laughing, I just did what he said...and I took a deep breath! I have to admit, he took just as good care of me as the nurses did. She even told him one day, "You get the Caregiver of the Year Award." He would have made a great doctor.

If you know anything about spinal cord injury, using the bathroom on your own is a *big* deal! I had to wear a catheter for about a month and once it was removed, I still had to have someone catheterize me. Occasionally, they would get me to try to go on an actual commode but to no avail.

One day, my nurse asked if I wanted to give it another try. She mentioned that it was probably hard to pee lying in a bed. There's a lot of truth to that. We're told over and over when we're little not to pee in the bed. So, instinctively, you just know you are not supposed to do that! So, I gave it another try.

Since arriving at the hospital, I had gotten over any inhibitions I may have had in the past. But regardless, it's just not easy to go with someone watching. By this time, I had an audience of two nurses and my mom in the room. This may sound crude, but I was stepping out in faith and I was going to do what I said I was going to do. I told my nurse, matter-of-factly, that I was going in there to pee in that pot! I was determined. I must have told them about ten times what I was going to do before we made it to the bathroom. It was mostly for my benefit, though. I was keeping my faith turned on. Then to set the stage, I made them close my bathroom curtain, turn up the volume on the television, turn on the water and to "talk amongst themselves."

While they were "talking amongst themselves," my nurse said to let her know when I was going. By the time she got that out of her mouth, I was yelling, "I'm going! I'm going!" You would have thought I had just won the lottery by our excitement. But, to me, it was bigger. I called Mike right away to tell him the good news. The nurses and techs would stick their heads in my door just to let me know they had heard the good news. I even called my pastors, Pastors David and Paige Divelbiss, to let them know. They had been to see me the evening before and prayed for my bladder to function normally. Glory to God! He is still the same yesterday, today and forever!

I don't know why, but it just seems like most of the funny stuff happened around the bathroom. So, here's another one. Remember, any inhibitions were history by now! My nurse helped me onto the bedside commode one day and then turned around and sat on the edge of my bed with her arms crossed, just looking at me, like a friend stopping by for a visit. So I just looked up at her and said, "Soooo…how's the family?" Seriously! How can someone crack jokes in the middle of such a predicament? God. Just God!

Sitting up for the first time was very weird. I expected to sit up on the side of the bed like normal, but I was shocked when they sat me up and I rolled back into the bed like a wet noodle. It felt like my spine had literally been removed. And I couldn't be above a 45-degree angle sitting or standing without my blood pressure dropping and causing me to nearly black out. I had to start wearing compression hose, ace bandages over the hose and an abdominal binder just to get out of bed.

To regulate my blood pressure and get me used to an upright position again, they put me on a tilt table. You are strapped to a table that elevates to an upright 90-degree angle. They would raise me up about 10 degrees at a time. Most days I could only make it to 45 degrees before my blood pressure would drop and I would have to be lowered.

Once I started getting a slight movement back in my legs, I would move them the best I could on the table to get the blood flowing. It seemed to help me stay up longer and I eventually made it to a standing position.

Sometimes, the Bride of Frankenstein would cross my mind while I was on the table. Not because of how I looked, but because of how the doctor would raise the operating table to an upright position. I was still glad, though, that there were no mirrors in front of me to compare myself to her. But that reminds me of another incident.

One morning, we were running a little late for therapy, so they had to dress me quickly to make it to my appointment. Isaiah 61:3 says to *put on the garment of praise for the spirit of heaviness.* So I chose to put on a garment of praise that morning. I chose to smile and be in a good mood. That may have been the same morning I told my nurse, "I think I'll just take the day off." Of course, she just laughed at me! It never hurts to try!

My PT came to get me, and off we went down the long hallway. I was smiling at people, saying good morning and being overly cheerful—*choosing* to be in a good mood. By the way, you *can choose* to do that just as easily as you can choose not to. My PT parked my wheelchair in the gym and it just happened to be right in front of a mirror. When I looked up, I said "Oh...my...gosh!"

She turned around quickly to ask what was wrong.

I said, "I cannot believe you let me go down the hall looking like this!" The Bride of Frankenstein had nothing on me! My hair was going *everywhere*! After we finally stopped laughing, I made her fix it. That was the last time I ever left my room without glancing in the mirror.

My first trip out of the rehab hospital was to visit my doctor, have x-rays done and check my progress. They had to load me, still in my wheelchair, in the back of a van and strap it down. It was a little scary driving through traffic this way, but we made it.

By the way, I had *the best* driver. After that day, every time she came by the rehab hospital, she would stop by my room to check on me and spend a few minutes brushing my hair, whether it needed it or not. Thoughtful things like that can mean the world to someone. Like my OT coming to the hospital on her day off just to bring her hairdresser to color my hair. Or my PT buying me a special pair of gloves on her way to work so I could turn the wheels on my wheelchair. Or my nurse bringing me home baked cookies. Sometimes the smallest things you can do for someone are actually the greatest.

Mike met me at the doctor's office because he wasn't allowed to ride in the van. As soon as I was situated, he went to the front desk to check me in and fill out the paperwork. While he was doing that, someone in the waiting room asked me, "Is that your dad?"

I held in the urge to laugh and just smiled and said, "No, he's my husband." They were a little shocked when I told them how old I really was.

Another time, I was in occupational therapy and an elderly gentleman, who I just fell in love with, asked me the same thing. "Is that your dad?" I did laugh that time because Mike was sitting there with me! He just smiled. He thought it was funny, too. I didn't realize I looked so young but most everyone thought I was in my twenties.

A nurse walked in my room one day, looked at me, looked at the chart, then back at me and left without saying a word. She went to the desk and told them she had the wrong room. She was supposed to see a forty-year old woman. They said, "That's her."

At each level of progression, I was looking around the gym for the next one. It was my way of keeping the vision in front of me. Every time I was raised up on the tilt table, I could see my next goal directly in front of me: the standing frame. It's a machine that holds your body in an upright standing position. I would watch intently from my table while someone else was in the standing frame, waiting for my day. And then it came!

On one occasion, my blood pressure was holding steady and I was able to stand up for almost ten minutes in the frame without passing out. I was laughing with my small audience when another PT walked over. He jokingly said, "I thought you were taller than that."

And again, before I had time to think, I said, "I thought you were taller until I stood up." We had another good laugh and he took it well. I believe laughter is what kept my blood pressure from dropping that day.

Proverbs 17:22, A merry heart does good, like medicine.

From the standing frame, I could see where I really wanted to be: the parallel bars. I passed it every day in the gym and could see it from every place in the room. It was my ultimate goal. I wanted on those bars!

One day we were at the standing frame and my PT asked if I was ready to give the bars a try. I said, "That's what I've been waiting for!"

Some days, I would have an audience watching and cheering me on. They were a huge encouragement and their excitement would rub off on me. Even the joking around was a blessing. It helped keep my mind off of my situation and push forward.

I was finally ready to take my first step on the parallel bars. I had a larger audience that day and we were even waiting for some of the staff to get to the gym because they wanted to watch. I think they were as excited as I was!

Someone suggested bringing the full-length mirror over so I could see. One of the PT's said, "Well, it ain't pretty!"

I let them know *real quick* that I didn't need the mirror. I said, "If a guy tells you something ain't pretty…it ain't pretty!" It's good to laugh.

Nehemiah 8:10, ...for the joy of the Lord is your strength.

WEEPING MAY ENDURE FOR A NIGHT

Psalm 30:5 (NKJV), Weeping may endure for a night, but joy comes in the morning.

It's good to have people on your side; people to laugh with...and cry with.

It wasn't all laughs, by any means. Most of the time, it was just a choice I made. We can choose to let the hard places get the best of us...or we can choose to let the best of us rise above those hard places.

It's hard to comprehend wanting to move and your body won't respond. Your mind knows what your body should be doing. It's telling it what to do but nothing is happening.

I remember trying so hard to move my legs while I was in ICU. I tried so hard that my mind believed I was moving my legs, like I was pedaling a bicycle. It felt so real that I asked Mom if they were moving. They weren't, but it felt so real to me that I just closed my eyes and kept right on pedaling.

I did laugh and smile a whole lot more than I cried. But even when I did cry, I refused to get out of faith and give up. Before I said anything, I made sure it didn't go against the Word of God. Our words are powerful. Make sure you are speaking the same thing God is speaking about your situation.

Proverbs 18:21 (NKJV), Death and life are in the power of the tongue, and those who love it will eat its fruit.

Mark 11:23 (NKJV), For assuredly, I say to you, whoever says to this mountain, 'Be removed and be cast into the sea,' and does not doubt in his heart, but believes that those things he says will be done, he will have whatever he says.

Matthew 12:37 (NKJV), For by your words you will be justified, and by your words you will be condemned.

I was in the hospital for two months and there were only three times that I really cried. I'm not bragging by any means. Believe me, there were times I had to fight it but I refused to let it get the best of me. And I couldn't have done it without Jesus.

The first time I cried, I was with Mike. I had just been moved to the rehab hospital and was getting settled in my room. He was always there with me but I still missed the closeness. I couldn't hug him or lay beside him and I needed that. I missed him. On top of that, I was just nervous about the whole situation.

I didn't want anyone to know I had been crying so I made him hurry and clean my face before the nurses came in. I wanted to be strong and I needed to look strong. For the most part I was, but I did learn that it's okay to cry. Sometimes you just have to let the pressure off so you can keep going.

Another time, we had just had a meeting with my nurses, techs, and physical and occupational therapists. I was expecting the meeting to be with two or three people but there must have been about a dozen people that came in my room that day, and it caught me off guard. Each person talked about my progress and the goals I had accomplished and what needed to be done. It was all good and encouraging but one thing that was said kept ringing in my ears. It was about my progress and therapy a year or two down the road; maybe even longer. Doing this years down the road was *not* in my plans. I didn't have time for this! *Don't they know that I'm walking out of this hospital?*

They finished and asked if I had anything to say or add but I couldn't think of anything because the two years was still ringing in my ears; that and the pressure pain from sitting in the wheelchair. All I could think of to say was that I was hurting and needed to relieve the pressure.

I knew that medically they were giving their prognosis but that was the last thing I had expected to hear. I think they were a little disappointed that I hadn't added anything but I had mentally shut down and just needed to hold it together until they all left the room. After all, I was trying to be strong, full of faith and always have a good attitude. And I couldn't let anyone know that I was just seconds away from losing it.

After everyone left, Mike stood me up to transfer me to the bed. He asked me why I didn't say anything in the meeting, but I couldn't answer him. I knew what would happen if I tried to speak and I was still trying to hold it together. But as soon as I put my arms around his neck for him to help me in the bed, I literally had a meltdown. Everything I had been holding in for two months came pouring out with such force that I had absolutely no control over it. I just stood there crying out, "I don't want to do this anymore! I don't want to do this anymore!"

He stood there holding me until I got it all out. He helped me in the bed and talked to me for a few minutes. Then he asked if I wanted to talk to one of my nurses who was also a pastor's wife. He went and got her, and she sat with me for a few minutes and really encouraged me. As soon as she walked out, my pastor walked in and ministered to me. That afternoon, I had a visit from a girl who had recently been discharged from the rehab hospital with a spinal cord injury. My nurse had asked her if she would stop by and visit with me one day when she was there for outpatient therapy. She just happened to be there on the one day I needed her most. She had a determination and a love for life that blessed me more than anything. She was so fun to listen to. I showed her that I had gotten slight movement back in one leg. She said, "Girl, you've got way more than I had!"

You can hear stories of people who have been through the same thing, but it doesn't compare to actually talking to someone face to face who has lived it; someone who understands where you are and what you're going through. I always knew I would be all right but after talking to her that day, I could *see* that I would be all right.

Before she left, she asked how old I was and I told her I was forty. She was a young girl just starting college and she thought I was about her age. That alone would make anyone feel better, no matter what they're going through!

I was scheduled to leave on a Friday, but a week before my discharge date I was asked if I would consider extending my stay for two more weeks. Since I was making really good progress they felt it would be beneficial, so I agreed to stay. It turned out to be the best decision because it was during those last two weeks that I started taking my first steps by myself on a walker.

I had seen people coming and going over the past two months and most were counting the days until they would go home. I was getting better and now I was the one counting the days. I missed being home with Mike and my girls. This was the reason for my last cry. Just a simple, "I miss my family."

I had been away from home for two months and I was ready to go home, but there was another part of me that was nervous about going home. I had people taking care of me constantly. I still couldn't bathe or dress myself or really do anything for myself. I had thought I would be farther along when I went home. I knew I was getting better. I no longer needed anyone staying with me at night, or during the day for that matter, but it was still comforting to have them there.

My mom and best friends had taken turns staying with me at night. Each night was something different: massages, facials, manicures, singing to me, watching movies together or just curling up on the foot of my bed to talk. Each one speaking words of life into me, encouraging me, standing in faith with me and praying for me. And I was always so happy to see them!

It reminds of the story in Mark Chapter 2. Four men were carrying a paralytic to Jesus, but there was no room in the house for them to enter. They went up on top of the house and let the man down through the roof. Verse 5 says, "When Jesus saw *their* faith…" This was not just the faith of the paralytic, but the faith of all five of them. That's what these women were to me. We all had the faith to overcome the situation, but they were also there to help carry me.

As special and treasured as each of these women are to me, there was still one person who lit up my heart and put a smile on my face like no one else could: my husband, Mike. When he walked in the room, he brought a strength with him that I could hold on to.

He took care of our girls at night and took them to school in the mornings. He wanted to make sure things stayed as normal as possible for them. Then he would drive to the hospital to spend the day with me, eighty miles round trip. I could look at the clock and know exactly when he would walk through my door. Not only did he feed me the Word of God every day to keep my faith built up, but he encouraged me to press through the hard places. "Don't give up. Show them you can do it."

For days he would sit at the end of my bed and say, "Move that toe!" I couldn't lift my head to see my toes because of the neck brace, but I trusted him to tell me what was going on.

Every day, "Move that toe! You can do it!" Then one day, he said, "You did it! You moved your toe!" We were so excited. I practiced moving that toe every day.

One day, I was able to look down at the end of the bed and see my toes. He said, "Move that toe!"

I tried to move it with everything I had and for the first time, I saw my big toe on my left foot twitch! I said, "I saw it move!"

Then, with a big smile on his face, he said, "That's the first time it's moved."

Hebrews 11:1 (NKJV), Now faith is the substance of things hoped for, the evidence of things not seen.

Romans 4:17, …even God, who quickeneth the dead, and calleth those things which be not as though they were.

If you had asked me what the most important thing your husband ever said to you was, I probably would have said the same thing most people say—I love you. But he said something to me that has meant way more. Don't get me wrong. I love you is still *way* up there and I like to hear it, but some things are just more valuable.

I was back home and getting around better. As I was helping to put the groceries away, my foot caught on the bottom cabinet door and I fell to the floor. Mike came over and knelt beside me to make sure I was all right. He could tell I was more frustrated than hurt, but still I was close to tears. He just looked at me and said, "Everything's going to be all right. I'm not going anywhere." To me, that sounds a lot like what Jesus said in Matthew 28:20…

WITH YOU ALWAYS

Matthew 28:20 (NKJV), … I am with you always, even to the end of the age.

God loves us so much and wants us to depend on Him. I found out just what that means. Being paralyzed puts you in a position of total dependence on God and on those who are caring for you.

I was feeling totally helpless one day. I had been left alone in my room for "privacy" and was told to press the call button when I was ready for the nurse to come back. She sent Mike out and put a *Do Not Disturb* sign on the door.

My call button had to be replaced with a touch pad because I couldn't use my fingers. They would place it beside my pillow so all I had to do was press my hand or arm against it.

A couple of minutes after they left, I was in pain and needed help. I went to reach for the touch pad, but it had been accidentally left on the table out of reach.

The door was closed so no one could hear me when I called out for help. I don't think I've ever felt as helpless as I did at that moment. No one would come until I buzzed for them and I was hurting more by the second. God was the only one Who knew I needed help, so I asked Him to send Mike in to check on me. About 30 seconds later, Mike opened the door and asked if everything was okay. I knew God had been with me through all of this, but at that moment, I realized just how much He *was* with me. When I found myself in the same situation another time, He immediately sent someone in to help me.

LEAN ON ME

It's easy to look at the big picture and wonder, "Will I ever get there?" But when you break it down, it's so much easier to get where you're going. We look at where we want to be and see our shortcomings, our inabilities and think there is no way to do it. It's too big! But if we take it one step at a time, we'll get there.

Psalm 37:23, The steps of a good man are ordered by the Lord, and He delights in his way.

I used to watch the other patients walking back and forth from their rooms to therapy when it was literally all I could do to push my wheelchair one inch at a time while these people were passing me left and right.

One day, my PT let me push myself back to my room. There was a little hill where the floor changed elevations slightly, and going over it just wasn't happening for me. I struggled and struggled and finally just had to stop and rest. I was close to tears when another PT walked by, looked around to see if anyone was looking, then quickly pushed me up the hill. After a heartfelt thank you, I took a deep breath and went right back to rolling my way to my room…one inch at a time.

A very dear friend of ours sent me a card while I was in the hospital with a note that read, *Daddy always said, "Life's hard by the yard but a cinch by the inch!"* I've kept that saying close to my heart. It has seen me through days when I would have rather just sat down and said, "That's enough. No more." But instead, I keep pressing forward. Jesus has already given us the victory to overcome every obstacle. Knowing that, how could I not keep going forward?

John 16:33 (NKJV), These things I have spoken to you, that in Me you may have peace. In the world you will have tribulation; but be of good cheer, I have overcome the world.

1 Corinthians 15:57 (NKJV), But thanks be to God, who gives us the victory through our Lord Jesus Christ.

1 John 5:4 (NKJV), For whatever is born of God overcomes the world. And this is the victory that has overcome the world—our faith.

They were still trying to get me used to being in an upright position. It was difficult because my blood pressure would drop within minutes and I would be close to passing out. It usually took every ounce of strength I had to do anything.

One day, they decided it was time to try the actual bathroom. After my two techs helped me settle in, they told me they would come right back as soon as I called for them.

My nurses, techs and therapists were amazing. It was no accident that I was placed in the care of these special people. God hand-picked them for me. They were not *just* hospital employees. They were ministers. They took care of me spirit, soul and body. Each one had something special about them, something that ministered to me every time we were together. They didn't refer to me as a hospital room number. They treated me like family. One nurse called me Princess and threatened to bring me a crown, with all the special treatment I was getting. Maybe I *was* a little spoiled. (And of course, my family thinks I still am!)

I hadn't been in the bathroom long before my blood pressure started dropping. I needed help back to bed before I passed out, but I couldn't get the call button to work. I asked God to send them back in to check on me, and they came right back.

By this time, my head was against the wall. They helped me up but I was too weak to move. I asked one of my *"ministers"* if I could lean on her. I put my head on her shoulder before she had time to answer. She said, "Go ahead and lean on me."

Standing there with both of them holding me up, I started singing, "Lean on me. When you're not strong..."

And they picked up the song from there. ... "I'll be your friend. I'll help you carry on. You just call on your sisters, when you need a hand. We all need somebody to lean on." I had my very own choir, and let me tell you, those ladies could sing!

The strength that had left my body started flowing back in. I stood up straight and lifted my hands toward Heaven, thanking God and giving Him the glory. They sang to me all the way back to the bed, holding me up and taking it one step at a time

Shortly after taking my first steps at the parallel bars, my physical therapist set a walker in front of my wheelchair so I could get a feel for it. I said, "That's what I've been look-ing for." I'm not sure how many times I practiced that day, whether it was a few times or just one, but I do remember taking a step. And then another. And then another.

Each day on the walker, my PT would get me to go a little farther than the last time. One day, she had me walk a few feet to the doorway of the gym. Then she asked, "Do you think you can make it to the next door?" When we reached that door, we would reach for the next one and then the next. Then she asked, "Do you think you can make it to the corner?" I decided when I reached the corner that I wanted to walk all the way to my room. It was really a long way for me but I wanted to do it. We were going small distances, one step at a time, with a tech following close behind with a wheelchair in case I needed to sit down. Honestly, it was overwhelming and I felt like I didn't have the strength to do it, but I wasn't going to quit.

2 Corinthians 5:20 says that *we are ambassadors for Christ.* That means we are representing Him and my life should reflect that. I was determined to represent Jesus as the Healer that He is. Just because my body was screaming at me, "You can't do this! Just sit down! Let them push you to the room!" I wasn't going to listen.

I was meditating on Mark 11:23 one day and I started thinking about the mountain in my own life and how big it was. In the natural, it just looked impossible. But I knew that with God all things are possible.

Matthew 19:26 (NKJV), But Jesus looked at them and said to them, "With men this is impossible, but with God all things are possible."

I love this one, too: *Jeremiah 32:27 (NKJV), Behold, I am the Lord, the God of all flesh. Is there anything too hard for Me?*

I began to picture an actual mountain in my mind with all the different levels leading up to the peak. Then I knew what I had to do to conquer this mountain I was facing. I had to do it one level at a time.

I was sharing this with one of my best friends, and she told me about a documentary she had seen on Mount Everest. In order for the climbers to reach the top of the mountain, they had to climb it one level at a time to allow their body to adjust to the changing altitude. Once they had adjusted to that level, they would ascend to the next.

Just like God had showed me to break my mountain down piece by piece, I was going to break this distance down the same way: inch by inch. I would pick a spot a few feet away and just focus on making it to that point. I fixed my eyes straight ahead and took it one step at a time, never taking my eyes away from the spot and not looking past it. When I reached that spot, I could see how much closer I was to conquering my mountain. I took a breath, picked another spot, fixed my eyes and took another step.

Sometimes things can seem overwhelming. Other times, they seem downright impossible! Just keep your eyes focused on where you're going. Don't focus on the problem and wonder how you can possibly go on. How will you ever get there? Just look at how far you've come and how much shorter the distance is to where you're going. Sure, you can look into the future and get overwhelmed, thinking, "It's too hard to reach that place." But God doesn't expect you to get there by yourself.

Joshua 1:9 (NKJV), Be strong and of good courage; do not be afraid, nor be dismayed, for the Lord your God is with you wherever you go.

Walking to my room that day was one of the hardest things I had tried to do. But I knew if I was going to make it, I needed to stand on God's Word. A very dear couple sent me this scripture while I was in the hospital:

Isaiah 40:31, But those who wait on the Lord shall renew their strength; they shall mount up with wings like eagles, they shall run and not be weary, they shall walk and not faint.

As each step got harder and I got weaker, that scripture came to me. I wasn't sure what the PT and tech would think about me quoting scriptures out loud, but I knew I needed help if I was going to make it all the way to my room. So I said out loud, "I shall run and not be weary. I shall walk and not faint." Then I heard a voice behind me say, "I can do all things through Christ Who strengthens me!" The tech following behind me with the wheelchair started quoting scriptures with me.

Let me tell you! The Word of God is alive and powerful! When she said that, a strength came over me and I knew I could do it! I made it to the mark and picked my next one, then the next one, both of us confessing the

Word of God all the way to my room. A huge milestone accomplished!

My legs were so fatigued from the walk that once I was in bed, my legs began to shake and tremble. They were literally bouncing on the bed. I've never seen anything like it! I wasn't in pain, so we weren't concerned about it. I just lay in the bed watching my legs for about ten minutes until the trembling slowly subsided.

I was determined that no matter what the prognosis was, no matter what I saw or how I felt, and no matter what wasn't moving, I was going to walk by faith.

There were times in therapy that I wanted to say that's all I can do but when I was asked if I could do one more set, I did. I was determined, and I was going to take God at His Word. *To let patience have its perfect work, that I may be perfect and complete, lacking nothing (James 1:4).*

Right before I was discharged, someone said to me, "Girl, you were bad off when you first got here!" I just laughed. If I was, I sure didn't realize it.

Even from the beginning, I told people I was going to walk out of that hospital. I couldn't even sit up without passing out, but I was using my faith and I was determined to do everything I could in the natural and let God take care of the supernatural.

You might be wondering how I could be thankful in such a hard place where I couldn't stand or walk on my own, or really do much of anything. It's the same as with any situation. We take things one step at a time.

Sometimes you just need to turn around and look how far those steps have taken you. There's always something to give glory to God for, no matter who you are and no matter the circumstance, big or small.

> *1 Thessalonians 5:18 (NLT), Be thankful in all circumstances, for this is God's will for you who belong to Christ Jesus.*

It says be thankful "in" all circumstances. Not "for" all circumstances. There is always something to be thankful for.

There were many nights I couldn't sleep and I would just lie there reflecting on life. I could have dwelt on the negative but I chose not to. Instead, I chose life.

> *Deuteronomy 30:19, …I have set before you life and death, blessing and cursing; therefore choose life, that both you and your descendants may live.*

Some nights I would pray. Some nights I would sing softly to myself. Some nights I would meditate on a scripture I had learned that day, being careful not to forget it.

Some nights I would imagine myself walking and running, going over in my mind what I would say to people, giving my testimony of what Jesus had done for me.

Even though I couldn't see much improvement with my physical eyes, I could see it with my spiritual eyes, and I would rehearse it over and over. Even though I was paralyzed, some nights I would lie in the dark, smiling from ear to ear!

My brother came to visit me one day with one thing on his mind: to kidnap me. He went to the nurse's station to get permission to take me out of the hospital. They put me in my wheelchair and he wheeled me outside. In the almost two months I had been there, I had only been outside the hospital one time and that was to see my doctor. That really couldn't be considered outdoors. I was taken straight from the building to the van and back inside. It had definitely not been enough time to enjoy being outside the hospital. It felt a little strange going outside. I was excited to be outdoors, but a little nervous at the same time. Then we were going down the sidewalk, away from the hospital, away from everyone.

He rolled me down just a little way from the building, put a pair of sunglasses on me and pointed me directly into the evening sun. Feeling the sun beaming down on my face was the most wonderful feeling. He stood there by my side, letting me soak in the warmth of the sun and enjoy the fresh, cool air for as long as I wanted. Why did he do that? Because that's just what big brothers do!

Since I was in a neck brace, I had to be bathed in the bed. I wanted a shower so badly, and even more than that, I wanted to wash my hair. I still had dirt and *things* in my hair from the accident. A shower was not an easy task for me but they knew how much I longed for one that they made it happen. They rolled in a full-length hospital shower bed to transfer me onto and then rolled me down to a huge shower room. I kid you not—I was so excited, I was giddy! After a month, it was absolutely heaven. I felt like crying, that's how wonderful it was. I asked if I could hold the shower nozzle. They briefly took my neck brace off for the first time and I just hugged the nozzle, letting the warm water pour across my neck.

Remember when I mentioned that I would tell people I was going to walk out of the hospital? A couple of days before I was discharged, one of the hospital staff stopped me in the hall and said, "I heard you've been telling everyone you're going to walk out of this hospital. Well, I'm going to let you walk out."

The day I was discharged, Mike and I were waiting for them to come get me, along with one of my best friends who was there with a video camera to capture the moment. I was excited to be leaving but also nervous about leaving the constant care.

In the distance, we heard singing and could tell they were coming down the hallway, getting louder and louder the closer they got. "Na-na-na-na..." Then they came in my room. "Na-Na-Na-Na...Na-Na-Na-Na...hey, hey, hey, goodbye!..." Everyone who had been working with me came to see me off, singing all the way to my room, finally handing me my long-awaited discharge papers!

They rolled me down the hall to the elevators and to the front doors of the hospital. Just as the automatic doors opened up, I asked the nurse to back me up so the doors would close. I wanted to make them open by myself. She gave me my walker and I walked out of the hospital all the way to my vehicle.

Mark 11:23 (NKJV), For assuredly, I say to you, whoever says to this mountain, 'Be removed and be cast into the sea,' and does not doubt in his heart, but believes that those things he says will be done, he will have whatever he says.

Those were just some instances that still make me smile.

CHAPTER 3

LOVE NEVER FAILS

Even in the middle of one of the worst situations imaginable, God was loving me. He made sure I had the best of everything: the best hospitals, doctors, nurses, physical therapists, occupational therapists, rehab technicians and everyone else who cared for me. He strategically placed the right people around me. Days when it seemed too hard, He had just the right person there to help. That is a loving God. That's a loving Father!

He loves us so much that He gave us His best—His only Son, Jesus.

John 3:16 (NKJV), For God so loved the world that He gave His only begotten Son, that whoever believes in Him should not perish but have everlasting life.

When I think about God's love, I think about a parent's love for a child. Parents want to give their children the best. They want them to have more opportunities and better lives than they had.

Matthew 7:11 (NLT), So if you sinful people know how to give good gifts to your children, how much more will your heavenly Father give good gifts to those who ask him.

How much more does God want the best for us? We want to be there to pick up our children when they fall. How much more does God want to be there for His children?

In the hard places, you have to make the decision that you're going to believe the Word of God, no matter what. Just because you're going through a rough time, it doesn't make it okay to be in a bad mood and stop walking in the love of God. And yes, your flesh will want to rise up and have a pity party.

My nurse was in the room with me not long after I was moved to the rehab hospital. We were talking and I must have had *the look* because she said she would give me ten minutes to have a pity party, but that was it. I decided to forego the pity party. A few weeks later, she was telling me a story about her life and I told her I'd give her ten minutes to have a pity party, but that was it. You know, it's really hard to have a pity party when you can make someone laugh!

I decided early on that I was going to show God's love no matter what. Just because my accident happened, it didn't change who I was. I was still a child of God, still an ambassador for Christ and still on this earth to share His love.

When you're in the hospital, usually the first thing the doctors and nurses want to know is how you're doing. I decided I would do the same thing. When they came in, I started asking how they were doing. Sometimes I'd just listen. Sometimes I'd ask if they wanted me to pray for them. I think I caught one of my doctors off guard one day because when I asked him how *he* was doing, he looked at me strangely—like he had never had a patient ask him that before. I could tell it meant a lot to him that I had taken the time to ask instead of it just being about me.

It's good to remind ourselves that it's not always about us. We all go through hard places and it could just be a kind word or smile that makes all the difference in the world. Helping someone in their trouble can sometimes be the very thing we need to help us through ours.

When you really live your life for God, people will notice that there's something different about you. Some may be encouraged by it. Some may just want to know if you're for real.

The Word of God is our life and it's what we do. We were fighting for my life and people were watching.

There was one particular person at the hospital who seemed to be drawn to me. She would always come by to check on me even when I wasn't on her rounds. Our upbringings were completely different and she was a lot younger than I was, but there was also something very special about her that I was drawn to. I think maybe God just put a love on the inside of me for her. Whatever it was, there was something special about her and I knew God wanted me to just love on her.

She had to stop by the hospital one day, and she came to visit with me for about an hour. She knew Mike and I were Christians because she had been watching us. She had even told her husband that they needed what we had. She had a lot of unanswered questions and didn't know if she believed in God. I didn't preach to her. I just listened. Then I told her that if she really wanted to know if God was real, ask Him to show her. Just say, "God, if You're real, I want to know." God began revealing Himself to her. I spoke to her about a year later and she had accepted Jesus as her Savior.

Loving people opens the door to be used by God and to be loved by others in return.

CHAPTER 4

PREARRANGED AND MADE READY

Have you ever looked back at some of the hard places in your life, the ones where you may have felt so far from God or wondered where He was, only to find that He was there the whole time? That He had already taken care of the situation before you ever got there? He had the answer before there was ever a problem. He knows our future better than we know our past.

> *Ephesians 2:10 (AMP), For we are God's [own] handiwork (His workmanship), recreated in Christ Jesus, [born anew] that we may do those good works which God predestined (**planned beforehand**) for us [taking paths which He **prepared ahead of time**], that we should walk in them [living the good life which He **prearranged and made ready** for us to live].*

> *Isaiah 46:10 (NLT), Only I can tell you the future before it even happens. Everything I plan will come to pass, for I do whatever I wish.*

I don't know about you, but that helps me! You can rest in that! I got a revelation of this when the Lord reminded me of something.

A few years ago, I heard a minister talk about how the fathers in the Old Testament would speak things into their children's lives, especially on their deathbeds. The children would be called to their father's bedside and he would bless them. The last thing they said to their children was always the most important.

It made me think about my dad who went home to be with the Lord in December of 2003. My first thought was… "I wasn't there. I was on a ski trip in Colorado with the church youth group."

On the morning of the ski trip, Mom called me. She was in the emergency room with Dad. Mike and I were just leaving so we stopped by the hospital first. He wasn't doing well and I had a hard decision to make. Stay with Mom or go with the youth group. We were leaving within the hour and it was too late to get someone to take my place as a chaperone. After talking to Mom, she assured me it was all right to go. There was nothing I could do by staying. I don't know how many times in the past our family had been *called in* to the hospital with my Dad but each time, he always recovered. I was just sure it would be the same this time. With her blessing, I made the decision to go.

Two days before we were to come home, Daddy went home to be with the Lord. And I was a thousand miles away. All of my family was gathered around his hospital bed, everyone except me. I felt regret so many times, that I should have been there. But God brought something back to my remembrance when I heard that minister speak.

About a week before the trip, Daddy was in the hospital in ICU, so I went to see him on my lunch break. The nurse had just brought in his meal and asked me if I wanted to feed him. She gave me instructions and left us alone. I went around the plate, giving him a bite of everything... *but...very careful* to skip over the carrots. One thing I knew about my Daddy, he did *not* like carrots.

He had been in the nursing home for a while due to dementia and strokes and sometimes I wasn't sure if he knew who I was. It was quiet in his ICU room and I started having those thoughts again. *"Do you know who I am? Do you remember me?"* I made a couple more rounds on the plate.

Why I did what I did next, I couldn't tell you. Maybe I was being ornery or maybe I was just "Daddy's little girl" wanting to cry out, *"Are you in there?"* But I did the "unthinkable!" I dared to go where no one in my family had ever dared to go! I scooped up the carrots and gave him a bite. I paused, watching his face intently, ready to bolt for the door if necessary, but I didn't get a reaction. I made another round on the plate and when I got back to the carrots, I scooped them up again. He ate them without complaining. I was disheartened. *My Daddy* would *never* eat carrots.

I stepped back into reality...the big girl...and this time, asked him if he wanted any more carrots. He didn't say much anymore, and hadn't said anything since I arrived. But he answered me and said two words that were very familiar to me, "Not particularly."

With a huge smile, I thought, "You *are* in there! You *are* still my Daddy!"

The nurse came in to finish up and she asked him if I was his daughter and he nodded. I kissed him goodbye and told him I loved him. When I stopped in the doorway, I looked straight at him and said again, "I love you, Daddy."

He looked at me and said with a determination to get each word out, "I…love…you."

The most important words a Daddy could ever say were my Daddy's last words to me. I didn't know that days later I wouldn't have my Daddy any longer and that that would be our last time together. But God knew.

Mike and I were talking one day about how God had started preparing us months, even years, before the accident ever happened. It's good to listen. God knows what's ahead.

We were children's pastors for twelve years. Loved it! Recommend it! I think we grew more in children's church than we did in "big church!" When it was time to start a new curriculum, I would ask Mike what subject he thought we should teach, and he would say, "I think we need to minister on healing again." It was just something he felt led to do frequently. It wasn't just the kids who were being ministered to. God knew we were going to need it, too.

God had also led Mike to start getting out of debt, so he was working diligently at it. We didn't know at the time how important it would be in the near future to have those debts paid off, but God did. He was preparing us for what was ahead. I was in the hospital for two months and now we were living on one income. Meanwhile, people were blessing us financially and bills were being paid off. Some bills were just cancelled. What could have been a huge financial hardship turned out to be nothing at all.

Mike and I had also started working out a few months before the accident and walking about two miles, three times a week. I didn't know how important strengthening my muscles would be, but again, God did.

In the hospital, I had been unable to stand up on my own and hold my weight. I had to use a sliding board and pivot my body to get from the bed, to the wheelchair, to the PT table for therapy. One day, I was lying on the table while my PT was stretching my legs. She held one leg and had me pull it in to my chest and then push out. I pushed out with everything I had and almost knocked her over with the strength in my legs. All those months of working out had prepared me for what was ahead.

A couple of weeks before my discharge date, I had a home evaluation where my physical therapist and occupational therapist came to our house to see what remodeling would need to be done to make sure I could get around in a wheelchair. This was my first trip home in two months. We had only been in our newly remodeled one-hundred-year old house about nine months when the accident happened, so I was ready to be home. Even if it was just for an hour or so.

I was thrilled when we pulled up to our house, and just as excited when I saw the wheelchair ramp that a close friend had built for me that looked more like a deck than a ramp. While he was at it, he had built a concrete pad to park our vehicle on so I could easily roll to the ramp in my wheelchair. As soon as I rolled through the door, I breathed in deeply. I could still smell the new wood in the house. It was like going in for the first time!

We weren't sure what kind of renovations to expect. They would need to make sure my wheelchair could get through the doorways and that nothing was in the way for me to get around. I made it in the front door. So far so good!

We tested all the doorways and made sure there was plenty of space to get around the furniture. They went down the checklist and found that everything had already been done. Since it was an old house, the doorways were wide, rooms were spacious and open and it was so easy to roll across the hardwood floors.

We had believed God for a house ten years before we ever moved. God gave us the desires of our heart and also made sure that it would be exactly what He knew we were going to need. Just another need He took care of before we ever got there.

If you're in the middle of a situation, just know that God has already prepared your victory before you ever reach the battle. You can count on it. Sometimes you'll see it as you're going through the hard place. Sometimes you won't see it until it's already past. But rest assured, it's taken care of!

Revelation 12:11 (NKJV), And they overcame him by the blood of the Lamb and by the word of their testimony, and they did not love their lives to the death.

I used to think I needed to be completely well and whole before I gave my testimony but I think it's just as important to testify while you're in the middle of a storm. People need to see you walk it out because the middle is where they need the most help.

There are a lot of things physically that I've had to relearn and some, I'm still learning. It's good to look back and remind yourself how far you've come. But don't be discouraged by where you are. Keep pressing forward. Besides, that's where the prize is!

Philippians 3:13-14 (NKJV), Brethren, I do not count myself to have apprehended; but one thing I do, forgetting those things which are behind and reaching forward to those things which are ahead, I press toward the goal for the prize of the upward call of God in Christ Jesus.

FAITHFUL

There's nothing quite like when you really get the revelation down on the inside that God loves you! That God really does love *me!*

Just knowing that should be enough to get you through anything! Then I found out that He *really* wanted to bless me, *really* wanted to answer my prayers, *really* wanted to give me the desires of my heart! Just because He loves *me!* I started using my faith for just about everything. If I had a need, I used my faith to believe Him for it. Whether it was money or a parking space, any request, big or small, I chose to believe God. Don't ever think that something is too small to ask God for His help. The small victories help build your faith to believe Him for bigger victories. And never forget the things He has done for you. They will remind you of His faithfulness. He did it then, He will do it now.

When we decided to start a family, it wasn't as easy as we thought it would be. Two and a half years later and still we had no children. After months and months, my doctor didn't know what was wrong. The next step was exploratory surgery, but we decided against it. A couple of months later, our pastor, Pastor Bill Bush, taught about how to get your prayers answered. I had heard this before, but that night was different. It was like he was talking to me and no one else was in the room. As soon as I got home, I wrote my prayer exactly the way I wanted to say it with every scripture promise I could find on the matter. Mike and I prayed in agreement that night for a baby. About nine months later, we had Michelle. Two and a half years later, we had Allie. There were other options we could have tried, but we decided to believe God.

When our marriage was in trouble, we could have gone for counseling. We could have given up. But instead, I asked God for help. Actually, I was *really* new at asking God for things so it was more like, "God, can you just fix Mike?" I just knew that if He fixed Mike, then everything would be fine. About six months later, I realized we were getting along better. Excited about my *new* husband, I mentally went down my checklist to see what

God had fixed. Nothing had changed. Then it dawned on me. I didn't have a *new* husband. Mike had a *new* wife! Mike wasn't the one God had been working on. He had been working on me! So much for thinking I had it all together! Once He got me headed in the right direction and doing what I was supposed to do, then He was able to work on Mike. When we both got in line with God, that's when our marriage really made a turnaround. Things started falling into place, and through the years, it just keeps getting better.

One day, early in our marriage, I needed to buy a few groceries but didn't have the money. Twenty dollars would get us through until we got paid on Friday. I decided to ask God for it instead of borrowing. That day at work, two people happened to pay back money they had borrowed from me. I was still a few dollars short but I still believed that God would get the money to me so I continued to thank Him for taking care of it. When I was getting in my car after work, I noticed a shopping bag on the back seat of my car with something I had bought that I really didn't need. I returned the item and had the rest of the twenty dollars for groceries.

I was waiting for some paperwork to come in the mail from the Office of Motor Vehicles. It wasn't urgent but I just wanted to take care of it before leaving on vacation. I called to find out when it would be arriving and the earliest I could expect it was 4-6 weeks. We were leaving in two weeks. So, I prayed that the paperwork would be hurried through the system. I checked the mail the first week and nothing. The thought would come that it's not going to be here in time just like they said, but I refused to doubt. I said, "In Jesus' Name, it *will* be here before we leave on vacation." I continued to check the mail every day expecting to see the letter. Two days before we left, the letter was in the mailbox! I didn't *have* to have the letter. But why pass up a great opportunity to believe God?

I used to dress up in costumes on a regular basis in children's church. I loved it! People never knew what I would come out wearing next. One of my regular characters was Gospel Granny. I wore a gray wig with a bun in the back, my grandmother's glasses and blue crocheted shawl over my great grandmother's pink double-knit dress, knee high hose and ankle high boots.

One Sunday, I was supposed to do a skit for the adult service. Earlier in the week, I had gotten sick and had been coughing for days. I was taking medicine, along with standing on the Word for my healing. When Sunday rolled around, I was still coughing. I had to perform in minutes and I didn't know how I was going to do Gospel Granny's voice without coughing. I didn't want to tell them I couldn't do the skit so I asked Mike to pray for me before I went into the church. I continued to cough all the way to the doors of the sanctuary.

When it was time for Gospel Granny to go in, I took a step of faith and walked through the doors, performed the skit and then exited. I didn't cough one time and I have to strain my voice to sound like Gospel Granny. As soon as I walked out of the sanctuary, the coughing started back. I didn't care! God had just showed up! I could have cancelled the skit (and I did consider it), but I made the choice to trust God.

All the times I had made the choice to believe God for things, when I really didn't have to, had strengthened my faith to believe Him when that was the only option I had. I was lying in a hospital bed, paralyzed from the chest down, couldn't use my hands and was barely able to lift my arms. There were no other surgeries, no medications, no home remedies—nothing to fix a spinal cord injury. My prognosis was that I would have to live with whatever I was left with after I recovered from the surgery. The *only* option I had *was* to believe God.

The time to start building your faith is not when the trials and calamities hit. The time to start is when things are calm and life is good. Use your faith to believe God for things. He loves you. It gives Him pleasure to bless you.

Luke 12:32 (NKJV), Do not fear, little flock, for it is your Father's good pleasure to give you the kingdom.

Psalm 35:27 (NKJV), Let them shout for joy and be glad, who favor my righteous cause; And let them say continually, "Let the Lord be magnified, Who has pleasure in the prosperity of His servant."

It's not just about the things. Of course, we may need the things but the main reason to believe is to build your faith. Put the Word of God in your heart now so when those storms do come, you're prepared. When you build up your spirit, it will sustain you.

Proverbs 18:14 (AMP), The strong spirit of a man sustains him in bodily pain or trouble, but a weak and broken spirit who can raise up or bear?

I'm thankful for the times I chose to believe God when I didn't have to. Seeing God's faithfulness helped me to remain steadfast and immovable.

1 Corinthians 15:58 (NKJV), Therefore, my beloved brethren, be steadfast, immovable, always abounding in the work of the Lord, knowing that your labor is not in vain in the Lord.

And in Romans 4:21, *being fully persuaded that, what He had promised, He was able also to perform.*

Not only should we be using every opportunity to build our faith, but we need to teach it to our kids. When Michelle was about five years old, she had stuffed a piece of tissue in her nose and couldn't get it out. It was wedged so far in there that she couldn't even blow it out.

Finally, I told her I couldn't get it and we only had two options. I could take her to the doctor, or we could pray and ask God to get it out. I knew the answer to that question before I even asked! She said she wanted to pray and let God get it out. She was *not* about to willfully volunteer to go to the doctor. We prayed and then I said, "Okay, hold one side closed and blow really hard." This was the same thing we had tried over and over to no avail. She took a deep breath, held one side closed and blew as hard as she could. That tissue shot out of her nose on the first try! We laughed so hard and praised God. To this day, you can't tell her that God doesn't answer prayers!

CHAPTER 5

WALKING ON HIGH HILLS

Habakkuk 3:19 (NKJV), The Lord God is my strength; He will make my feet like deer's feet, And He will make me walk on my high hills.

The title for this book comes from this scripture. It means that just as steady and sure as a deer is at dangerous heights, so are we when it comes to any trouble, challenge or responsibility.

Habakkuk 3:19 (AMP), The Lord GOD is my strength [my source of courage, my invincible army]; He has made my feet [steady and sure] like hinds' feet and makes me walk [forward with spiritual confidence] on my high places [of challenge and responsibility].

God has already established our steps. He upholds us with His righteous right hand and will not let us fall. He makes us to *walk*, not to stand still, not to stay in the middle of it, but to *walk* on our high hills right into the victory He's already planned out on the other side.

This scripture also has a two-fold meaning for me. I've read it many times but one day, the very last word jumped out at me and I saw it like this. *He will make me walk on my high heels!* Granted, it's not talking about shoes but technically, you *are* standing on a hill! I got excited anyway because I have really missed my high heels! I've missed cute shoes in general, but especially my high heels.

Shoes will either make or break an outfit and one of the hardest things to shop for has been *cute* shoes that are safe for me to walk in. Cute flats with ankle straps (to keep them from slipping off my feet and tripping me) have been few and far between.

Mike has known my struggles and also how much I've missed my high heels, so he told me that *when* (not *if*) I can walk in heels again, he will fly me to the Jimmy Choo shoe store in Atlanta and buy me any pair of shoes I want. I already have my pair of bright red high heel pumps picked out.

Jeremiah 32:27 (NKJV), Behold, I am the Lord, the God of all flesh. Is there anything too hard for Me?

Not at all.

4 KEYS TO STAYING IN FAITH

Staying in faith is one of the most important keys to walking in victory. Jesus told the woman with the issue of blood in Mark 5 that her faith had made her whole. He told the blind man in Mark 10 that his faith had made him whole. He told the leper in Luke 17 that his faith had made him whole. In Matthew 15, He told a woman that her faith had made her daughter whole. If their faith could make them whole, then our faith can make us whole.

> *Matthew 21:21-22 (NKJV), So Jesus answered and said to them, "Assuredly, I say to you, if you have faith and do not doubt, you will not only do what was done to the fig tree, but also if you say to this mountain, 'Be removed and be cast into the sea,' it will be done. And whatever things you ask in prayer, believing, you will receive."*

With faith being so important to our victory, I have four keys to give you that have helped me personally to stay in faith. Well, actually I have five, but number five is a pair of red high heel pumps and that may not be your thing! I encourage you to get your own "number 5!"

1. REPRESENT CHRIST

> *2 Corinthians 5:20 (NKJV), Now then, we are ambassadors for Christ...*

As an ambassador, I want to represent Christ for Who He is—the Healer.

*1 Peter 2:24 (NKJV), who Himself bore our sins in His own body on the tree, that we, having died to sins, might live for righteousness—by **whose stripes you were healed.***

2. PLEASE GOD

Hebrews 11:6 (NKJV), But without faith it is impossible to please Him, for he who comes to God must believe that He is, and that He is a rewarder of those who diligently seek Him.

Above all else in this life, I want to please God. This one scripture alone lets me know that if I'm not in faith then I'm not pleasing Him. No matter what a situation looks like, no matter how you feel, no matter what the report says, believe God to change it. Not only does it please Him when we're in faith, it pleases Him to be our rewarder.

3. IT'S TEMPORARY

2 Corinthians 4:18, While we look not at the things which are seen, but at the things which are not seen: for the things which are seen are temporal; but the things which are not seen are eternal.

Temporal, in the Greek means for a season, enduring only for a while, temporary.

Philippians 1:6 (AMP), And I am convinced and sure of this very thing, that He Who began a good work in you will continue until the day of Jesus Christ [right up to the time of His return], developing [that good work] and perfecting and bringing it to full completion in you.

James 1:4 (NKJV), But let patience have its perfect work, that you may be perfect and complete, lacking nothing.

Bringing it to full completion—perfect and complete, lacking nothing. If that's not calling a situation temporary, I don't know what is.

4. DON'T GIVE UP

2 Corinthians 1:20 (NKJV), For all the promises of God in Him are Yes, and in Him Amen, to the glory of God through us.

If all the promises of God are yes and amen...*and they are*...then it's already yours. Sometimes it's right away—sometimes there's a waiting period. Why is it that we are more patient when we have to wait on natural things but when we ask God for something, we expect it immediately? If it doesn't come when we think it should, we give up or think it must not be His will. If He promised it in His Word, then we can rest assured that it's His will.

Think about this. What if your miracle was just around the corner but you gave up too soon? When I get to Heaven one day, I don't want to find out that

God had my miracle all planned out but I gave up and walked away. Just because we don't see it when we think we should doesn't mean the answer is no or that the provision is not there. If God promised it in His Word, then the answer is yes and amen. When we do what the bible says, we get bible results.

> *Hebrews 6:11-12 (NLV), We want each one of you to keep on working to the end. Then what you hope for, will happen. Do not be lazy. Be like those who have faith and have not given up. **They will receive** what God has promised them.*

> *(NKJV) …imitate those who through faith and patience inherit the promises.*

God loves you. He wants the best for you. He has a hope and a future for you. He is not withholding anything from you.

> *1 Corinthians 15:58 (NKJV), Therefore, my beloved brethren, be steadfast, immovable, always abounding in the work of the Lord, knowing that your labor is not in vain in the Lord.*

He has given us everything we need to be more than conquerors in this life.

2 Peter 1:3 (NKJV), as His divine power has given to us all things that pertain to life and godliness, through the knowledge of Him who called us by glory and virtue.

Romans 8:37 (NKJV), Yet in all these things we are more than conquerors through Him who loved us.

Stay in faith…Don't give up. God had your victory planned out before you ever had the problem.

Psalm 139:16 (NLT), You saw me before I was born. Every day of my life was recorded in Your book. Every moment was laid out before a single day had passed.

Galatians 6:9 (NKJV), And let us not grow weary while doing good, for in due season we shall reap if we do not lose heart.

Hebrews 10:23 (AMP), Let us seize and hold tightly the confession of our hope without wavering, for He who promised is reliable and trustworthy and faithful [to His word].

Hebrews 12:2 (NKJV), looking unto Jesus, the author and finisher of our faith, who for the joy that was set before Him endured the cross, despising the shame, and has sat down at the right hand of the throne of God.

HINDRANCES TO YOUR FAITH

Along with staying *in* faith, there are two things we need to guard against *hindering* our faith. One is our thoughts. There's a saying that goes, *the mind is a terrible thing to waste,* but not controlling it and letting it run wild is much worse! We can't allow our thoughts to be contrary to the Word of God. What you are thinking and meditating on will eventually get in your spirit and you'll start believing it.

> *Proverbs 23:7 (NKJV), For as he thinks in his heart, so is he.*

And what you believe will eventually come out of your mouth.

> *Proverbs 18:21 (NKJV), Death and life are in the power of the tongue, and those who love it will eat its fruit.*

3 KEYS TO GUARDING YOUR THOUGHT LIFE

1. RENEW YOUR MIND TO THE WORD OF GOD

> *Romans 12:2 (NKJV), And do not be conformed to this world, but be transformed by the renewing of your mind, that you may prove what is that good and acceptable and perfect will of God.*

> *(NLT), Don't copy the behavior and customs of this world, but let God transform you into a new person by changing the way you think. Then you will learn to know God's will for you, which is good and pleasing and perfect.*

Get in the Word and find out for yourself what it says about your situation. Don't just take someone else's word or experience on the matter. Find out the truth for yourself.

2. THINK ON THESE THINGS

> *Philippians 4:8, Finally, brethren, whatsoever things are true, whatsoever things are honest, whatsoever things are just, whatsoever things are pure, whatsoever things are lovely, whatsoever things are of good report; if there be any virtue, and if there be any praise, think on these things.*

If what you are thinking about does not fit in or agree with that list, then it doesn't need to be in your thoughts. Replace it with the Word of God.

3. CAST DOWN IMAGINATIONS

> *2 Corinthians 10:3-5, For though we walk in the flesh, we do not war after the flesh: (For the weapons of our warfare are not carnal, but mighty through God to the pulling down of strong holds;) Casting down imaginations, and every high thing that exalteth itself against the knowledge of God, and bringing into captivity every thought to the obedience of Christ.*

Thoughts are going to come. But it's up to us whether we meditate on them or not.

If what we're thinking about does not line up with the Word of God, cast it down. Throw it out. Replace those thoughts by speaking what God's Word says about the situation. Your victory has everything to do with what you are thinking, believing and speaking.

FEAR NOT

Fear is the second thing we need to guard against hindering our faith. When fear is present, faith is absent.

Mark 4:35–40 (NKJV), On the same day, when evening had come, He said to them, "Let us cross over to the other side."…And a great windstorm arose, and the waves beat into the boat, so that it was already filling. But He was in the stern, asleep on a pillow. And they awoke Him and said to Him, "Teacher, do You not care that we are perishing?" Then He arose and rebuked the wind, and said to the sea, "Peace, be still!" And the wind ceased and there was a great calm. But He said to them, "Why are you so fearful? How is it that you have no faith?"

Luke 8:50 (NKJV), But when Jesus heard it, He answered him, saying, "Do not be afraid; only believe, and she will be made well."

Mark 5:36 (NKJV), As soon as Jesus heard the word that was spoken, He said to the ruler of the synagogue, "Do not be afraid; only believe."

Fear will rob us of the promises of God and we can't allow it to have any place in our lives.

In the first chapter, I mentioned the scriptures that I spoke over myself at the accident. The first one the Holy Spirit gave me was *2 Timothy 1:7 (NKJV), For God has*

not given us a spirit of fear, but of power and of love and of a sound mind.

I honestly believe that taking authority over fear that day had everything to do with me walking again. I had a split second decision to make: be in faith or be in fear. I didn't know what I was facing, but I did know that whatever it was had to be done in faith, and fear could not be allowed to operate. However, after I returned home, fear slowly tried to creep in.

I had settled back into a somewhat normal routine: out-patient therapy and helping Mike with our girls and the house as much as I was able. But one thing I was not comfortable with was getting in a vehicle. Accidents can sometimes leave you a little shell-shocked and you'd just rather not go anywhere if at all possible.

For a long time, I was only comfortable riding with Mike and it was especially hard allowing our girls to ride with anyone else. I prayed for God's protection continuously but the uneasiness was still there. The *what ifs* had entered my thought life and my prayers were more out of fear of what could happen than they were in faith to what He had already promised. I thought I was just being cautious, but fear was inching its way in and the only way to put a stop to it was by renewing my mind *again* to His protection and faithfulness. The anxious and worried thoughts were then replaced with the peace of God and a confidence that our God is faithful to do as He promised.

Philippians 4:6-7 (NKJV), Be anxious for nothing, but in everything by prayer and supplication, with thanksgiving, let your requests be made known to God; and the peace of God, which surpasses all understanding, will guard your hearts and minds through Christ Jesus.

Hebrews 10:23 (NKJV), Let us hold fast the confession of our hope without wavering, for He who promised is faithful.

A few years later, Allie was the passenger in a vehicle accident. They were struck by an oncoming vehicle causing it to flip over and land upside down on its roof. Hanging upside down, Allie unbuckled her seat belt, flipped over and crawled out of the broken window. Both her and the driver were miraculously unhurt—not even a scratch. He Who promised is faithful!

Being a Christian does not make us exempt from trials and hardships. It does, however, qualify us for victory every time!

Psalm 34:19 (NKJV), Many are the afflictions of the righteous, but the Lord delivers him out of them all.

CHAPTER 6

THE ROAD TO RESTORATION

Your challenge could be a spinal cord injury, a cold or losing a job; whatever the circumstance, life is just altered from the norm. Your victory depends on how you look at your situation. If you see yourself staying in that place and never getting out on the other side, you're basically living without hope. Why not look at it another way?

Imagine driving along a two-lane interstate and you are in the right lane. The left lane is bumper to bumper, yet they are steadily passing you, headed to the same destination you are. Just up ahead, a sign says *lane ends, merge left*. You try to get over, but there are cars for miles and you have no way to get over. Now your lane has ended, and all you can do is sit idle, watching the cars go by. You're stuck. You happen to glance to the right and realize there *is* a way out—an exit. Now you have a choice. *You* have a choice. No one else can make it for you. *You* are the driver. *You* are the one behind the wheel. *You* are the one in control of your destination.

You can stay where you are, hoping someone will let you in. You can even stay right where you are, watching the cars steadily pass you by, wishing you could be where they are. Or…you can take the exit. But it is going take a lot longer than the interstate due to the back roads and lower speed limits. Going off the beaten path may even be a little bumpy from all the potholes. You can expect a few curves in the road. You'll have to pay more attention to the road because you could encounter a hairpin turn or two. More than likely, you're going to come across construction, detouring you onto yet *another* route. As if that's not enough, you'll need to keep a sharp look-out for those unexpected obstacles, like a dog or deer darting out in front of you. Or if you're in the south, the 'possum or armadillo.

I know how frustrating it is watching everyone pass you, but it's all in how you look at the road you're traveling. Yes, taking the long way is not always your first choice. It will take longer to get where you're going, but one thing you can count on: you *will* get there. I've learned that taking the exit, the back roads, the scenic route, is a much more enjoyable drive. There's more to see and experience than you ever would have by taking the interstate that will get you there more quickly.

I used to do things really fast. I worked fast. I walked fast—*really* fast! I had a to-do list pages long. Some days, it was all I could do to keep up with it. I remember running down hallways to keep up with what I needed to get done. On one of those occasions, I tripped and literally slid like I was coming into home plate. I was getting things done quickly, but it sure wasn't worth the rug burns I got! Or the things I was overlooking. Sometimes those "things" were people. You don't realize how much is passing you by until you're forced to slow down.

Whether it's the devil throwing up a road block or just wrong choices on our part, God always has a plan and a way out.

*1 Corinthians 10:13 (NLT), The temptations in your life are no different from what others experience. And God is faithful. He will not allow the temptation to be more than you can stand. When you are tempted, **He will show you a way out** so that you can endure.*

Life will throw you curves but you don't have to handle them alone. God promised He would never leave you nor forsake you. In Luke 8:22, Jesus said, *"Let us go over to the other side."* All we have to do is get in the boat with Him. We *are* going over to the other side.

Have you ever made a wrong turn and ended up in the wrong place? Did you have to drive all the way back home and start over? No. You just looked at a map to get you back on course or let your GPS reroute you from the very spot you were at right then. No matter where you are, you can get where you're supposed to be from where you are now—at this very moment.

You might think that you've lost a lot of valuable time. Just leave that to God. He can redeem the time and turn any situation around.

Romans 8:28 (NLT), And we know that God causes everything to work together for the good of those who love God and are called according to His purpose for them.

Things are different in my life now. Certain things have to be done a little differently than before. I definitely look at life a lot differently. But you know what? I can honestly say that I love my life more now than I ever did before. God literally turned my situation around, and I sure do love Him for that!

God has the same destination for all of us. In Jeremiah 29:11, He called it a future and a hope. We may not all get there the same way, but with Him, we will get there. If you will invite Him, He will turn your situation into a journey so amazing that you never could have imagined it. He will put you in places that you never could have reached on your own. He will put you in people's lives that you never would have met otherwise. The very thing that God brought you out of is the very thing that He wants to use you in to be someone else's miracle.

I know that I don't have it all figured out, but I'm confident that God does. As long as He is directing our steps, everything is going to be all right.

Hebrews 13:5 (NKJV), …For He Himself has said, "I will never leave you nor forsake you."

Final Exhortations

1 Corinthians 16:13-14 (NKJV)
Watch, stand fast in the faith, be brave, be strong.
Let all that you do be done with love.

ABOUT THE AUTHOR

Peggy Pedroza has served alongside her husband, Mike, in nearly every aspect of the local church for over 20 years, including the area of their first love, children's ministry. Peggy resides in Louisiana where she is a devoted wife, mother of two and an encourager to many.